SEVEN

PILLARS

OF

WISDOM

Angie Meadows

Wisdom has built her house.; she has set up its seven pillars. Proverbs 9:1

Study based on the NIV version. KJV answers are in parentheses.

A Thousand Tears, LLC
PO Box 1373 Huntington, WV 25715
rockofrecovery.com
enablersjourney.com
Rockofrecovery.1@gmail.com
Rock of Recovery Podcast Link:
https://feed.podbean.com/rockofrecovery/feed.xml

BUILD YOUR HOUSE

Turn you page sideways and build your house with seven pillars. Make the "fear of the Lord" your foundation and "wisdom" your roof.

Contents

INTRODUCTION

Many, many precious mornings I have spent with the Lord in His Word. When I first made a commitment to arise early, I would set an alarm for 4:30 a.m. It was rough getting my eyes open. Slipping downstairs in the quiet morning, I studied the Bible at the breakfast table. It was a chore and a discipline.

These wee morning hours started with drudgery. But soon, oh very soon, God would meet me there. I would pop out of bed before my alarm and couldn't wait to hear what the Lord would say to me that morning. These times became my secret delight.

In seeking Him, I found Him! The mornings went from drudgery to excitement. O the depth of the riches both of the wisdom and the knowledge of God! How unsearchable are his judgments, and his ways past finding out!

Seeking the Lord gave me rich insights. When I would find a passage that intrigued me, I would ponder it throughout the entire day. When I thought I understood it, I would be amazed to get even deeper insight.

One morning I read Proverbs 9:1, "Wisdom has built her house, she has set up her seven pillars." This verse piqued my curiosity, and I could not stop thinking about it. Two years later, I was still pondering this verse and praying over it. Suddenly, I felt compelled to read and re-read the chapters surrounding the verse. It took many months to find 7 concepts that could be pillars. Could we have found God's 7 pillars to wisdom? Discernment (insight), truth, righteousness (honest), knowledge, instruction, prudence and understanding became pillars to me. The fear of the Lord became the foundation of my house. Wisdom became my covering.

As we search out hidden treasures from God's Word, we will surely find many more precious jewels to fill our house. But for today, let's build our house on a solid foundation.

TEACHING TIPS

I taught this study to 8–10-year-old children. There were 15-20 children in the class, each one found their verse and marked it with a sticky note under it. Each younger child had an older child beside them. The question would be asked, and the older child would help the younger child find the answer. Soon the younger children could find their own verse and the answer quickly and with confidence. By the end of the study, the older children were doing word searches and writing me studies. The moment I see frustration, I step in and point to the word in the Scripture that is in the answer. Or I ask another student to help them a bit.

When we do word searches or Bible studies like these, our hands will be in the Word of the Lord, and we will be seeking his wisdom and learning his ways. Then the Holy Spirit will empower us and ignite a fire in our hearts and what was once a chore will become a delight. Persevere! The rewards are great and lasting riches.

Lesson One: Have the participants draw their house as they find the pillars. The foundation is the fear of the Lord and Wisdom is the roof or the covering. Be sure to make 7 pillars and name them as you find them in lesson one.

Lesson Two: Observe the outline and develop outlines as you go along and let the Lord help you pull out jewels from his word.

CHAPTER ONE

WISDOM'S 7 PILLARS

Pillar is a firm upright support for a superstructure.

Find Wisdom's 7 pillars.

1. Proverbs 9:1 Who built the house?

    How many pillars are there?

2. Proverbs 9:4 What kind of person is wisdom seeking?

    Simple means young or not trained in wisdom. A person who is easily led astray.

3. Proverbs 9:5 What does it mean to eat and drink with wisdom?

4. Proverbs 9:6 Find pillar 1. What does wisdom tell them to do?

5. Proverbs 7:7 Can you find pillar number 2?

6. Proverbs 8:7 Find Pillar 3. This is the hardest one to find.

If we are wise, what will we speak?

What is wickedness (abomination)?

Should foul (crooked or perverse) language ever come out of our mouth? Lying, cursing, evil words, gossip, back talking, etc.

7. Proverbs 8:8 Find pillar 4. Wisdom's words are what?

What is not in a righteous man's mouth?

Righteous means free from guilt or sin.

8. Proverbs 8:9 Find pillar 5.
God's Words in the Bible are called wisdom's knowledge. This wisdom is like what to them with uprightness (understanding) and knowledge?

If a person doesn't believe in the Bible, would they be a wise man?

9. Proverbs 8:10 Find pillar 6.

What is better than silver?

What is better than gold?

10. Proverbs 8:12 Find pillar 7.

Prudence means careful good judgment that allows someone to avoid danger or risks; the ability to govern and discipline oneself using reason.

Who lives with prudence?

11. Proverbs 8:17 Who does wisdom love?

Who shall find wisdom?

12. Proverbs 9:10 What is the beginning of wisdom?

What does it mean to "fear the Lord"?

What is the blessing of finding wisdom?

Wisdom Self-Evaluation	
1. Can I avoid danger?	
2. Do I see evil coming and avoid it?	
3. Do I use wise words when I speak?	
4. Do I seek God's Word for knowledge and understanding?	
5. Do I have prudence? Prudence is the ability to govern or discipline myself.	
6. What would it look like if I was disciplining myself?	
7. Do I love wisdom?	
8. Do I fear the Lord?	

?

Prayer

Dear God,

Thank you for your Words of wisdom. Help me as I grow spiritually to have understanding, discernment, and insight. Let me know truth from a lie, to walk in righteousness and honesty with integrity, to have knowledge to walk in your ways and teach them to others. Make your Words plain and easy for me to understand. Help me to recognize when I am getting instructions from others and receive it willingly. Help me to govern my actions carefully, purposefully and to discipline myself. Help me to have good boundaries and to confess my sins frequently. Bless me with good friends and wise teachers. Let me walk in reverence and respect in the fear of the Lord. In Jesus name, Amen.

Answers

1. Wisdom
     Seven
2. Simple
3. Close fellowship or friendship
4. Leave (forsake) simple ways (foolishness) and live and go the way of insight (understanding).
5. Notice (Discernment) This means being aware of what is going on around you.
6. Truth. (Wisdom is speaking.)
     Truth,
     Something that causes disgust or hatred,
     No.
7. Just (righteous)
     Crooked (forward) or perverse words.
8. Knowledge,
     Right; (faultless)... very clear and easy to understand,
     No, the wiser a man becomes the more God's Words will be plain and right (faultless) to him.
     A man with unbelief has a sinful (evil) heart. (Hebrews 3:12)
9. Instruction,
     Instruction,
     Knowledge.
10. Prudence,
     Knowledge and discretion
11. I, wisdom, love them that love me.
     Those that seek me shall find me.

12. The fear of the Lord.

> It means to have reverence or respect for the Lord.
>
> Reverence, respect, awe or fear of God is in our hearts.

Memory Verse

Wisdom has built her house; she has hewn out its seven pillars.

CHAPTER TWO

WISDOM

Wisdom – accumulated knowledge; the ability to discern inner qualities and relationships: Insight; good sense; Judgment; a wise attitude or course of action. Antonym-foolish

Knowledge - the fact or condition of apprehending truth or fact. Antonym-ignorance

Discretion – cautious and reserved in speech; the ability to make responsible decisions.

Froward – habitually disposed to disobedience and opposition.

Perverse – turned away from what is right and good; corrupt. *Definitions from Merriam-Webster Dictionary

In Proverbs the Bible **personifies** "Wisdom". To personify something means to represent something as a person or to give it human qualities.

1.   Proverbs 9:1 Whose house can we live in?

2. Proverbs 9:10 What is the beginning of Wisdom?
   What does it mean to "fear" the Lord?

3. Proverbs 8:13 What does Proverbs 8:13 say the "fear of the Lord" means?

4. Proverbs 8:11 Wisdom is better than what?
   Is there anything as good as wisdom?

5. Proverbs 8:17 Who is speaking in this verse?
   Who does wisdom love?
   Who will find wisdom?

6. Proverbs 9:8b How will a wise person receive wisdom?

7. Proverbs 9:9 What does a wise man need to become wiser?
   What does a just (righteous) man need to increase learning?

8. Proverbs 9:11 What is the blessing of seeking wisdom?

9. Proverbs 2:1 What are the two instructions for us in this verse?

10. Psalm 119:97; Psalm 1:2 How do I hide commandments within me?

11. Proverbs 2:2 What are we to listen to?

    How could I apply my heart to understanding? (Secret is in verse 2:3,4)

12. Proverbs 2:4 What is wisdom likened unto?

13. Proverbs 2:6 Who gives wisdom?

    What else comes with wisdom?

14. Proverbs 2:7 What does God have stored up for us?

    If we walk blameless (upright) what does God become to us?

15. Proverbs 2:8-9 What are 5 ways He becomes a shield for us?

16. Proverbs 2:10 What will be pleasant to you if wisdom has entered your heart?

17. Proverbs 2:11 What will God give the wise to protect (preserve) them?

18. Proverbs 2:12-16 What kinds of things will wisdom deliver us from?

Answers

1. Wisdom
2. The fear of the Lord is the beginning of Wisdom.
       To fear the Lord means to reverence Him or respect Him.
3. The fear of the Lord means to hate evil, pride, and arrogance, and the evil way (bad behaviors), and a forward mouth (perverse speech).
4. Rubies
       No, nothing can compare to her.

5. Wisdom
   Wisdom loves those that love Her.
   Those that seek Her early (diligently).
6. Rebuke – Reprimand or to criticize sharply.
7. Instruction

Teaching

8. My days will be multiplied, and my years will be increased.
9. Accept (receive) my words and store (hide) my commands within you.
10. Meditate on them day and night.
11. Wisdom

Call out, cry aloud, look and search. This is done through prayer. Wisdom is Christ. If we seek Christ, we will find Him. If we pray and ask Him, He will give us wisdom.

...no good thing will He withhold from them that walk uprightly. Psalm 84:11

If any of you lack wisdom, you should ask God, who gives generously to all without finding fault, and it will be given to you. James 1:5

12. Silver and hidden treasure
13. The Lord

Knowledge and understanding

14. Victory (sound wisdom)

Shield (buckler)

15. 1) He guards (keeps) us. 2)Protects (preserves) the way. 3) He gives us understanding of what is right (righteousness) and just (judgment). 4) Then you will understand fairness (equity) 5) You will know every good path.
16. Knowledge
17. Discretion
18. Wicked men: 1) with perverse (forward) words. 2) who leave the straight (upright) paths 3) who walk in darkness 4) who delight to do wrong (evil) 5) who rejoice in perverseness of evil (forwardness of the wicked) 6) whose paths (ways) are crooked 7) who are devious (forward) in their ways (paths). Also, wisdom will protect us from an adulteress (strange woman) and wayward wife (stranger) with seductive (flattering) words.

Review

1) What is the fear of the Lord?
2) Wisdom is better than what?
3) How do I hide commands in my heart?
4) What blessing does following wisdom give me?
5) How can I find wisdom?

Prayer

O God,

Teach us your wisdom. Help us to understand your instructions. Place within our hearts a hatred for evil, arrogance, pride, and perverse speech. Show us our pride and help us to be intentional about humbling ourselves. Let us cherish your Words as a great treasure. Place within us a desire to lift our voice and cry unto you for wisdom, to meditate upon your words, and hide them in our hearts. O Gracious Heavenly Father, grant us humility to receive instruction and correction that we may grow in wisdom. In Jesus Name, Amen

Outline

<u>Fear of the Lord</u>

- Judgment
- Protection
- Right living
- Equity (fairness)
- Good path
- Shield

WISDOM REPELS

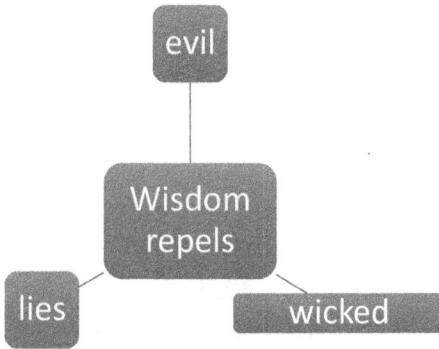

Wisdom
- Better than everything
  - Silver
  - Gold
  - Hidden Treasure

Blessings
- ❖ Long life

<u>My Responsibility</u>

- Cry – lift our voice (pray)
- Seek
- Receive instructions
- Teaching
- Love wisdom
- Seek early (diligently)
- Accept
- Reprove/Rebuke
- Hide commandments
        Love wisdom

Memory Verse

Long life is in her right hand; in her left hand are riches and honor. Proverbs 3:16

CHAPTER THREE

FEAR OF THE LORD

Reverence - honour, or respect: deference.

1. Psalm 34:7 Where does the angel of the Lord encamp?

    Why is the angel of the Lord there?

2. Psalm 34:8 Who is the blessed/happy?

3. Psalm 34:9 God provides for whom?

4. Proverbs 3:7 Should we think of ourselves as wise?

    What should we do?

5. Proverbs 23:17 If I recognize envy in my heart what do I need to do to correct it?

6. Proverbs 24: 21 If we fear God, with whom are we not to associate?

7. Proverbs 29:25 What is the opposite of the fear of the Lord?

    What will be the results of the fear of man in your life?

    What will be the reward of the fear of the Lord?

8. Proverbs 3:25 If horrible/destructive things happen should we be afraid?

   Look at verse 26 for the "secret" to not being afraid.

9. Psalm 118:4 Those who fear the Lord say what?

10. Psalm 118:5 What do we do when we are in anguish?

11. Psalm 118:6 When we truly trust God and know he is by our side then what will we never fear?

Discern those individuals who do not fear God

12. Psalm 36:1-3 Find five clues to help you recognize a man with "no fear" of God?

13. Psalm 55:19 How can I know if a person doesn't fear God?

14. Ecclesiastes 12:13 What is the whole duty of man? (Find 2 things)

Answers

1. The angel of the Lord is near those who fear Him. The angel is there to deliver them.

2. The man who takes refuge (trusts) in the Lord is blessed.

3. God provides for those who fear Him.

4. No, we should not think of ourselves as wise. Instead, we should fear the Lord and shun evil.

5. I need the "fear of the Lord" to correct my envy and to be zealous for God. Zealous means to be fervent or actively seek God.

6. If we fear God, we will not join with the rebellious.

7. The fear of man is the opposite of the fear of the Lord. The fear of man is a snare. The reward for having the fear of the Lord is that we are kept safe.

8. No, we are to have no fear of sudden disaster or ruin that overtakes the wicked. The **secret** to not being afraid is to allow the Lord to be our confidence.

9. Those who fear the Lord say **His love endures forever.**

10. We cry (call) upon him, and He will set us free (in a large place).

11. I will not fear what man can do unto me.

12. The wicked have no fear of God. The wicked (1) flatter themselves and (2) cannot detect or hate their sin. The (3) words of their mouth are wicked and deceitful. They (4) are not wise and (5) don't do good.

13. A person who doesn't fear God, doesn't change.

14. The whole duty of man is to (1) fear God and (2) keep His commandments.

Review

1. Who does the angel of the Lord camp around?
2. Should we think of ourselves as wise?
3. If I fear the Lord, will I hang out with rebellious (disobedient) friends?
4. Those that fear the Lord say (finish the sentence), "His love endures....".
5. What should I do if I am in distress?
6. Should I be afraid of men (peer pressure)?
7. What is my duty?

Prayer

Father God,

Give us the "fear of the Lord" the ability to know you and to reject wickedness. Help us to detect our sin and repent quickly. Give us the confidence to stand strong against the world or any peer pressure to do evil. Let us zealously run after you. Loose our tongues to cry out to you when we need you. Set us free from the burdens of this world. Give us the ability to trust you in all circumstances. Make us wise enough to discern people with no fear of God. Help us to see what needs changed in our lives and to ask for your help to change it. Let us fear you, O God, and keep your commandments. Make your commandments plain and give us a heart to obey. In Jesus Name we pray, Amen.

Outline

Promises for those who fear the Lord

- The angel of the Lord will camp around us
- He will deliver us.
- He will provide for us.
- He will set us free (in a large place).

What are my instructions or responsibilities?

- Fear the Lord
- Take refuge in the Lord (trust)
- I am not to think of myself as wise
- I am to not be afraid of disaster
- I am to cry out to him when I am in trouble
- I am to let the Lord be my confidence
- I am to obey his commandments
- I am to shun evil.

Warnings

- Fear of man is a snare.

Recognition of a person who doesn't fear the Lord
• They don't change.
• They flatter themselves. (Could this look like boasting?)
• They cannot detect or hate their sin.
• Their words are wicked and deceitful.
• They are not wise.
• They don't do good.

Remember two things

1) I will not fear what anyone can do to me.
2) His mercy endures forever!

Memory Verse

Fear of man will prove to be a snare, but whoever trusts in the Lord is kept safe. Proverbs 29:25

CHAPTER FOUR

BLESSINGS OF THE FEAR OF THE LORD

Blessing-is an approval or encouragement.

1. Proverbs 14:26 How is the fear of the Lord described?

   What is the blessing for children?

2. Proverbs 22:4 What is the character trait coupled with the fear of the Lord?

   What are the blessings of humility with the fear of the Lord?

   Application: Compare and contrast earthly riches to heavenly riches.

3. Psalm 31:19 What fruit of the Spirit has God stored up for those who fear Him?

4. Psalm 31:20 Where shall he hide them?

   What is he hiding them from?

5. Psalm 33:18 Where is the Lord's eye?

What is the attitude of those who fear the Lord?

6. Psalm 85:9 What is near those who fear the Lord?

   What dwells in the land with us if we fear the Lord?

7. Psalm 103:11 How great is His love (mercy) upon them that fear Him?

8. Psalm 103:12 What does this love (mercy) do for us?

9. Psalm 103:13 Who does he have compassion on?

10. Psalm 103:17 How long will God's love (mercy) endure towards me if I fear Him?

    How will my children and grandchildren benefit?

11. Psalm 103:18 What is the condition to my children receiving this mercy?

12. Psalm 115:11 What is the command to those who fear the Lord?

    What is the blessing for trusting in God?

13. Psalm 115:13 What will the Lord do for me if I fear Him?

14. Psalm 115:14 Who else will partake of my blessing?

15. Psalm 145:19 If I fear the Lord, what two things can I expect according to this verse?

Answers

1. The fear of the Lord is a secure fortress (strong confidence).
    The children will have a place of refuge.
2. Humility is a character quality we need to intentionally develop.
    The blessings are riches, honor, and life.
3. He stores us goodness.
4. God hides us in the shelter (secret) of his presence.
    He hides us from accusing tongues (strife of tongues).
5. God's eye is upon those who fear Him.
    Attitude is hope.
    They hope in His unfailing love (mercy).
6. Salvation is near those that fear the Lord.
    God's glory dwells in the land with us.
7. His love (mercy) is as great as the heaven is high above the earth.
8. God's love (mercy) removes our sins from us as far as the east is from the west.
9. God has compassion (pity) on those that fear Him.
10. God's love (mercy) will endure from everlasting to everlasting. My children and my children's children will have his righteousness.
11. They must not forget to keep his covenant and remember to obey (do) his commandments.
12. The command is for us to trust him. The blessing I will receive is that God, himself, will be my shield and help.
13. God will bless me.
14. My children shall be blessed more and more.
15. He will fulfill my desire, hear my cry, and save me. When we fear the Lord and fellowship with him and fully give him our hearts. We will have the righteous desires he wants us to possess.
    *The only desire David had at the end of his life was God. See Psalm 73:25

Review

1) How is the fear of the Lord manifested in our life?
2) What is the character trait that will be prominent in a person's life if they fear the Lord?
3) What fruit of the Spirit is given to those who fear God?
4) How great is God's love (mercy) for those who fear Him?
5) What are two things my children must not forget if they want to receive my blessings?

Prayer

Blessings dear Heavenly Father,

We thank you for your Word that directs and guides our lives. Give us humility and the fear of the Lord. Hide us in your secret place from the strife of tongues. Protect us and save us. Be our shield and our help. Guide us to remember to cry unto You. Place within our hearts the desires you have for us. Bring salvation to our homes. Bless us and our children (current and future children) to remember your covenant and to obey your commands. Let us have a strong confidence in you, our Lord and our Savior. In Jesus name, we pray. Amen.

Outline

Blessings

- Place of refuge for my children.
- Riches, honor and life.
- Goodness (fruit of the Spirit)
- Hidden in the shelter of His presence.

- His eye is upon me.
- Salvation is near
- Protection from accusing tongues.
- His glory will be on our land.
- His love (mercy) will be as high as the heaven above the earth.
- Our sins will be as far as the east is from the west.
- He will have compassion (pity) on us.
- His love (mercy) will endure forever.
- My children and grandchildren will have His righteousness
- He is my shield.
- He is my help.

Character
- Humility

My responsibility
- Purpose to build a secure fortress (strong confidence) in the Lord.
- Choose to trust the Lord.
- Exercise my hope in His unfailing love.
- Keep covenant
- Obey and do His commandments
- Teach these things to my children and grandchildren.

Memory Verse

Proverbs 14:26 He who fears the LORD has a secure fortress (strong confidence), and for his children it will be a refuge.

Ponder
When you take your last breath on this earth, what will really matter?

CHAPTER FIVE

UNDERSTANDING

Understanding- a mental grasp: comprehension.

1. Proverbs 4:1 What is our instruction?

2. I Kings 3:9 What does Solomon pray for God to give him?
    .

3. 1 Kings 3:10 Did this please God?

4. 1 Kings 3:12-13 What blessings did God give Solomon?

5. 1 Kings 3:14 What is the if, then statement?

6. Proverbs 1:2-6 Why did Solomon write proverbs?

7. Proverbs 2:2-3 What is our instruction if we want understanding?

8. Proverbs 2:4-5 What will we find if we search and seek for understanding?

9. Proverbs 3:1 What are we not to forget?

10. Proverbs 3:2 What's the promise?

11. Proverbs 3:3 What are we to never let leave us and where are we to keep them?

12. Proverbs 3:4 Then what shall we win (find)?

    Favor with who?

13. Proverbs 3:5 When something happens, I don't understand, I am to do what?

14. Proverbs 3:6 Instead of fretting, I am to do what?

15. Proverbs 3:7 What do I need so I won't trust in my own wisdom?

16. Proverbs 8:5 What kind of heart do we need?

17. Luke 24:25 Why does Jesus rebuke the people in this verse?

18. Luke 24:45 In order for the disciples to understand, what did Jesus need to do for them?

19. Ephesians 1:18 What is Paul's prayer for us?

20. Philippians 4:7 Describe a heavenly understanding?

21. Philippians 4:6 What are the three secrets to acquiring this heavenly understanding?

Answers

1. Listen, pay attention
2. Discerning (understanding) heart
3. Yes
4. Riches and Honor
5. **If** Solomon walks in God's ways and keeps His statutes and commandments, **then** God will give him long days.
6. So, we could (2) attain (know) wisdom, discipline (instruction), **understanding** words of insight (understanding), (3) acquiring a disciplined life to do what is just and fair (justice, judgment, equity) (4) to give prudence to the simple, to give young men knowledge and discretion, (5) let the wise listen and add to their learning, and let the discerning get guidance, (6) for **understanding** proverbs and parables, the sayings and riddles of the wise.
    If we read one proverb a day everyday corresponding to the day of the month, we will read through proverbs twelve times a year. If we repeat this every year, we will have the ability to understand right from wrong and the ability to counsel others.
7. **To turn our ear to wisdom and apply our hearts** to understanding.
8. We will understand the fear of the Lord and find the knowledge of God.
9. Wisdom's teaching. (We are to keep the commands in our heart.)
10. Long life and prosperity
11. Love and faithfulness (mercy and truth). We are to bind the commands around our neck and write them on our heart.
12. Favor and good name (understanding). God and man.
13. Trust in the Lord with all my heart and lean not to my own understanding.
14. Acknowledge him and let him straighten (direct) my path.
15. Fear of the Lord.
16. Understanding heart. (The simple he speaks to are those who are untrained or young.)
17. Slow of heart and unbelief in Scripture.
18. He opened their (spiritual) eyes so they could understand.
19. He prays that the eyes of our heart (understanding) be enlightened, that we will know the hope of our calling, and the riches of the glory of our **inheritance** in the saints.
20. A heavenly understanding is the peace of God that transcends all understanding.

21. (1) Do not be anxious about anything.

    (2) Give everything to God with prayer and petition.

    (3) Be thankful.

    * Gratefulness is a key to decreasing anxiety.

    * A faithful prayer and trusting God with the outcome of life brings peace.

Review

1. What are spiritual eyes?
2. What is the heart condition that is dangerous?
3. What is a practical way to write the Word on my heart?
4. What are the secrets to having heavenly understanding?

Prayer

Dear God,

Thank you, Lord, for this study. Enlighten our spiritual eyes. Give us an understanding heart of wisdom. Help us to overcome anxiety through praying and becoming grateful for all things. Give us a believing heart. Teach us the fear of the Lord. Amen.

Outline

My Responsibility

- Hear
- Pay Attention
- Apply my heart to understanding
  Instructions:
- Lay hold of God's Word
- Keep Commandments
- Don't forget his Words
- Don't be anxious
- Give everything to God with prayer and petition
- Be thankful

Blessings

- Long Life
- Riches and Honor

Memory Verse

Give me understanding, and I will keep your law and obey it with all my heart. Psalm 119:34

CHAPTER SIX

DISCERNMENT (INSIGHT)

Discernment- The act of being able to grasp and comprehend what is obscure. A keen intellectual vision.

Synonym: Discrimination, perception, penetration, insight

1. Proverbs 7:7 What two types of people are in this verse?

> This simple person lacks common sense or good judgment. Read through the rest of Chapter 7 and see what the young man is doing that indicates he lacks good judgment.

> > What is Solomon's instruction to the young man is verse 24?

> > Where does this path lead in verse 27?

> > ## Application: What area of my life lacks good judgment?
> > Am I following anyone or anything more closely than Christ?

2. Hebrew 4:12 How is the Word of God described?

What can the Word do?

What does it mean to divide the soul and spirit?

Truth: *The more I am in the Word the more it becomes like a mirror to show me the evil in myself. There are thoughts and attitudes that keep my soul and spirit in conflict. I can recognize this conflict by doublemindedness and confusion.*

Application: What attitudes do I need to work on? (Anger, self-pity, selfishness, unkindness, etc.)

3. Hebrews 5:11 What is wrong with the people?

4. Hebrews 5:12 When God needs teachers those who are dull of hearing need what?

5. Hebrews 5:13 We need to be skillful in what?

6. Hebrews 5:14 So how do we get trained (mature enough) to discern right and wrong?

What things in your life are dulling your hearing and senses to the Word of righteousness?

Insight: *I exercise my senses daily through studying the Word of God and listening to preaching to increase my faith. (Romans 10:17) This is called strong meat or solid food.*

Application: Do you diligently persevere in quiet times with the Lord even when you don't feel like it?

Do you run to God when you stumble and sin? Or do you run away?

7.   I Corinthians 2:14 What are the two types of people?

How can we know the things of God?

8.   1 Corinthians 2:14 What are God's Words to a person without the Spirit of God?

9.   1 Corinthians 2:6-7 What kind of wisdom does God want to give us?

10. I Corinthians 2:16 Can we have the "mind of Christ?"

11. I Corinthians 2:5 What is my faith not to rest on?

What is my faith to rest on?

12. Proverbs 2:11 What will preserve (protect) us?

What will keep us?

13. Proverbs 3:21 What am I to keep before my eyes?

14. Proverbs 3:22 What blessings will wisdom and discretion be to me?

15. Proverbs 3:23-25 Outline the continual blessings and God's purposes for wisdom and discretion.

16. Proverbs 3:26 What is powerful enough to keep me from being afraid?

Answers

1.   Discerning and Simple. The writer of the proverb noticed (discerned) the situation.

     Following an adulterous woman

     Listen, pay attention.

     Wounded, grave, chambers of death.

2.   Living (quick), and active (more powerful) and sharper than a double-edged (two-edged) sword.

     Penetrate (piercing) the soul and the spirit.

     Judges (discerns) thoughts and the attitudes (intentions) of the heart.

3.   Slow to learn (dull of hearing)

4.   To be taught the basics all over again.

5.   The Word of righteousness

6.   By eating the solid food of the Word and training ourselves constantly to discern good/evil.

7.   A man with the Spirit and one without the Spirit.

     The things of God are spiritually discerned.

8.   Foolishness

9.   Secret (mystery), hidden wisdom

10. Yes

11. Men's wisdom

     Power of God

12. Discretion

     Understanding

13. Sounds judgment (sound wisdom) and discernment (discretion).

14. Life to me (my soul) and grace to my neck.

15. Walk safely, will not stumble, no fear, sleep sweet, not afraid of sudden fear/terror(disaster)/desolation(ruin) from the wicked.

16. The Lord is my confidence. And He keeps my foot from being taken (snared).

Review

1.   What are two types of people according to Proverbs 7:7?

2.   What does it mean to be dull of hearing?

3.   How do we prepare ourselves for the strong meat of God's Word?

4.   Can I just read God's Word and understand it?

5.   If my faith is weak, how do I get more faith?

6. What are some of the blessings God has for a person who seeks wisdom and discernment?

Prayer

May each of you have discernment and good judgment. May you follow the path which leads to God and quickly recognize any deceptive path that would lead you astray. May you be skillful in the Words of Righteousness. May you walk in the Spirit and develop the mind of Christ through diligent and persistent seeking of Christ our Lord and Savior. May your faith rest in the Power of God (even when it is tested by fire (I Peter 1:7). May God grant you the continual blessings of discernment: walking safely, not stumbling or the power to get up quickly if you do stumble, no fear especially of wicked men, restful sleep, no fear or threats of disaster or ruin from the enemies of God. And may discretion be life to your soul and an ornament of grace to your neck. In Jesus Name, Amen.

Outline

With Discernment

- Listen
- Pay attention
- Spiritual man
- Judging and discerning all things
- Mind of Christ

Without discernment:

- Simple-unlearned
- Led astray
- Lacks morals
- Lacks good judgment
- On the wrong path
    - Dull of hearing
    - Needing to be taught again

Walking in the Spirit

- United soul and spirit (purposefully following Christ)
- Developing the Fruit of the Spirit: Love, joy, peace, patience, kindness, goodness, faithfulness, gentleness, and self-control

Blessings

- Life to my soul
- Walking safely
- Not stumbling
- No fear
- Sweet sleep
- Not afraid of disaster
- Not afraid of the wicked

Memory Verse

I have more discernment (insight) than all my teachers, for I meditate on your statutes. Psalm 119:99

CHAPTER SEVEN

TRUTH

Truth - the body of real things, events, and facts.

1. John 1:14 Who was the Word?

    And with what is he filled?

2. John 14:6 Who is the way, truth, and life?

    In Verse 14:5 Thomas is saying he doesn't know the way. If you feel lost, Jesus tells us, "I am the way!" So, follow Jesus.

3. John 15:26 Who is coming to us?

    In John 14:16-17 Jesus asks for us to receive the Counselor (Comforter) also called the "Spirit of Truth". To receive this precious Spirit, we must obey His commandments. In verse 14:21, we are to love Jesus, then we shall be loved of the Father and Jesus will love us and show (manifest) himself to us.

4. John 16:13 Who will guide us into all truth and show us things to come?

5. John 17:17-19 What will truth do?

    Sanctification: means to separate from a profane for a sacred use; to be consecrated wholly to the service of God.

6. John 17:21-22 Why do we need sanctified?

    Verse 20-22 Jesus is praying for us to become one with Him and the Father. He uses the example of himself and God as one.

7. John 8:32 What sets us free?

    If we feel bound in our sin and troubles, we should pray for truth. Sin is bondage and holds us captive. Jesus sets us free. The world says freedom is to be able to sin. But True freedom is freedom not to sin.

    Find the secret of how to receive this truth is in John 8:31.

8. John 8:44 Who is not in the truth?

    Who is the father of lies?

    When we lie, who are we following Jesus or Satan?

9. Proverbs 6:21; 3:3; 7:3. Where are the three places to bind truth?

    Proverbs 6:22 In this verse, the commands of father and mother's teachings are emphasized. Commands will lead us when we sleep, keep us safe when we wake, and commands shall talk with us. What are some ways to write the Word of God on the tablets of our heart?

10. Psalm 119:105;130 What is Word likened unto to?

11. Psalm 119:151 Verse 151 says the Lord is near us, find the secret in verse 148.

12. Ephesians 5:8-9 What is produced in us, if we walk as children of the light?

13. Ephesians 6:14-18 What is the belt in our armor?
              What are the other pieces of our armor?

14. 2 Timothy 2:15 How can we know the truth of God?

        As we study God's word the Spirit of Truth will guide us, and we will be able to "rightly divide the truth" (KJV) which means to correctly explain the truth.

15. Revelations 21:8 Will we inherit heaven, if we are a habitual liar?

16. Proverbs 26:28 When I lie to someone what am saying to them?

Answers

1. Jesus.
Grace and Truth.
2. Jesus.
3. The Counselor (Comforter) called the "Spirit of Truth"
4. Spirit of truth.
5. Sanctify us – set us apart.
6. To become one with Christ
7. Truth. If you hold to Jesus's teachings (continue in His Word).
8. Jesus is talking to the religious leaders of his day. Satan. Satan.
9. Upon our heart, around the neck; upon the fingers.
10. Lamp; light for our path; and the Word gives understanding.
11. Meditating on God's promises throughout the night.

12. Goodness, righteousness, and truth.

13. Truth.

> Breastplate of righteousness; feet fitted with the gospel of peace; shield of faith; helmet of salvation; Sword of the Spirit which is the Word of God; and prayer and supplication; watching with perseverance and supplication for all saints... then we shall be able to open our mouths boldly to make known the mystery of God.

14. Present yourself is translated as "study" His Word in the (KJV) translation of the Bible.

15. No, liars aren't in heaven.

16. I am saying that I hate them.

> This is a very sobering study. We were born liars. It is only the Holy Spirit that helps us understand and walk in truth. Today, I want to teach you to pray truth by turning the Scriptures around and praying them.

Prayer

Thank you, Lord Jesus, that you became flesh and dwelt among us. Fill us with your grace and truth. Let us not only come but let us follow and abide or dwell in you as you dwell in the father. Give us, we pray, the Spirit of truth to counsel and comfort us. Sanctify us by Your Words. Set us apart for your use.

Give us the heart to continue in your Word. Let truth set us free. Free from sin and bondage. Let us bind truth upon our hearts, around necks and tie truth upon our fingers.

Give us the ability to focus and meditate upon your truths and not upon ourselves or our problems. O God, let your truth lead us, keep us and talk with us.

Let us purposefully place upon ourselves the armor of God. The helmet of salvation, the breastplate of righteousness, the strong belt of truth, the shoes to walk in peace and carry the gospel a mighty double-edged sword and a shield of faith which is the Word of God.

When we meet others with struggles grant us the ability to correctly explain the Word of God. Help us to plant Your Words in us so deeply that when we open our mouth the truth that lives in us comes forth and brings light and life to others. In Jesus Name, Amen.

Outline

Jesus is the Word and is full of grace and truth.

Jesus is the way, the truth, and life
The Spirit of Truth is the Comforter, the Holy Spirit.

Sanctify us – set us apart to use us for your glory.

Continue in God's Word:
The opposite of continuing in the truth of God's Word is walking in fear, unbelief, lying and growing cold in the Lord.

Three places to keep Word
• Upon our heart
• Around our neck
• Upon our fingers

▌*If we aren't abiding in God's Word, what are we be abiding in?*

- Confusion
- Depression
- Fearfulness
- Loss
- Anxiety
- Double mindedness

▌*Yield to Holy Spirit's Lamp and let him through the Word light your path.*

Purposefully develop Fruit
- goodness
- righteousness

▌*Develop fruit by planting truth so deeply in your heart, that you are free. Free to choose not to sin.*

Memory Verse

But the Counselor, the Holy Spirit, whom the Father will send in my name, will teach you all things and will remind you of everything I have said to you. John 14:26

CHAPTER EIGHT

RIGHTEOUSNESS

Righteousness — Acting in accord with divine and moral law; free from guilt or sin. Think of doing what is "right".

1. Isaiah 64:6 What is our righteousness likened unto?

2. Romans 5:17 What gift does God have for us?

    Romans 5:18 What did this one-man (Jesus) righteousness do for us?

    Justified means to treat us worthy of salvation.

    Romans 5:20 When sin abounds (increases), what happens?

    Romans 5:21 How does grace work?

3. I Corinthians 1:30 Who has God made Jesus to be unto us?

4.   A. 2 Corinthians 6: 4-5 Name the trials of Paul?

B. 2 Corinthians 6:6-7 What did the Holy Spirit provide for them?

C. 2 Corinthians 6:8-10 What are Paul's victories over his circumstances?

** This is what faith in God's righteousness can do for you.

D. So how could Paul receive all these blessings? Secret is in verse 3.

5.   A. Philippians 1:9 What is Paul praying for his fellow believers?

B. Philippians 1:10 Paul wants them to be able to understand what is good and be sincere and to be without what?

C. Philippians 1:11 How can we be without offense?

       D. Philippians 1:12 Paul tells us what God will do with the evil things that happened to us if we respond properly.

6.   A. 2 Timothy 3:16 How did we receive the Scriptures?

            B. 2 Timothy 3:16 Why did God give them to us?

7.   2 Timothy 4:7-8 If I continue with Jesus and keep the faith what is my reward?

8.   A. Titus 3:5 Are we saved by works of righteousness?

            B. Titus 3:5 How does He do this?

9.   A. Hebrews 12:10-11 What produces a harvest of righteousness and peace in our lives?
        B. Hebrews 12:10 Why would the Lord discipline (chasten) us?

        C. Hebrews 12:3 What should we do when we are chastened?

        D. Hebrews 12:11 How will we know our home is established in righteousness?

10. A. James 1:19-20 What is the instruction in verse 19?

            B. What does God say about the "anger (wrath) of man"?

11.   A. James 2:20 What two things are necessary?

        B. James 2:21 How was Abraham justified?

        C. James 2:22 How was Abraham's faith made perfect?

        D. James 2:23 What was credited (counted) as righteousness with God?

12.   Isaiah 32:17 What great blessings do we receive if we walk in righteousness?

13.   Isaiah 61:10 When the Lord is done with us, how shall we be clothed?

14.   A. Psalm 85:10 Who is the sister to love?

        B. Who is the sister to righteousness?

Answers

1.   Filthy rags
2.   A. The gift of righteousness.
     B. Christ's righteousness gave us justification unto life.
     C. Grace increased (abounds).
     D. Grace reigns through righteousness unto eternal life by Jesus Christ our Lord.
3.   Wisdom, Righteousness, Sanctification (holiness), and Redemption.
4.   A. Troubles (afflictions), hardships (necessities), distresses, beatings (stripes), imprisonments, riots (tumults), labors, sleeplessness (watching), and hunger (fasting).
     B. Purity (pureness), Understanding (knowledge), Patience (long-suffering), kindness, sincere love (love without hypocrisy), truthful speech (Word of truth), power of God, and the weapons (armor) of righteousness.
     C. Glory (Honor) over dishonor, bad report, and good report, genuine (truth over lies), guarded as   imposters, dying yet we live on, beaten (chastened) and not

killed, sorrowful, yet always rejoicing, poor yet making rich, having nothing and possessing everything.

D. Paul would put no stumbling block in anyone's path, so that the ministry wouldn't be discredited.

5. A. That their love would abound more and more in knowledge and in all judgment (discernment).

B. Blameless (offended).

C. If we are filled with the fruit of righteousness.

D. Advance (further) the gospel.

6. A. They were God breathed (inspired by God).

B. For teaching (doctrine), rebuking (reproof), correcting and for training (instruction) in righteousness.

7. A crown of righteousness.

8. A. No, but according to His mercy He saved us.

B. He did this by the washing of rebirth (regeneration) and renewing us by his Holy Spirit.

9. A. Chastisement/Discipline.

B. So we may share in his holiness.

C. We are to endure it and don't lose heart.

D. There will be peace.

10. A. Quick to listen (swift to hear), slow to speak and slow to become angry (wrath).

B. Man's anger will not bring the righteousness of God.

11. A. Faith and deeds (works).

B. By works... offering Isaac.

C. By obedience.

D. Belief. Faith/belief and good works/obedience are all pieces to fit together to make a person righteous.

12. Peace, quietness, and confidence (assurance).

13. God will clothe me in a garment of salvation covered with a robe of righteousness.

14. A. Faithfulness

B. Peace

Prayer

Heavenly Father,

We humble ourselves before you and acknowledge that our righteousness is like filthy rags. Justify us by Christ's work of redemption. We pray for Christ's robe of righteousness to be placed upon us. Let grace increase in our lives from you towards us and from us towards others. Give us the breastplate and impenetrable armor of righteousness that we may be able to make right decisions and walk uprightly.

When we are experiencing persecution, suffering and afflictions, give us extra grace to understand how to follow you more closely. Help us to recognize when we take an offense and refuse it and trust you in all things.

Fill us with the fruit of righteousness and let us abound more and more in your love. Circumcise our hearts that we may no longer walk in the flesh but walk in the Spirit of our living God. Let mercy, truth, righteousness, and peace be with us wherever we may go. In Jesus name we pray, Amen

Outline

- There is no righteousness in the flesh.
- We have a calling
- We are saved through faith evidenced by good works.

Gifts from God

- Justification
- Robe of Righteousness
- Faith
- Grace
- Crown of righteousness

Trials of Faith

- Troubles (Afflictions)
- Hardships (Necessities)
- Distresses
- Beatings (Stripes)
- Imprisonments
- Riots (Tumults)
- Hard work (Labors)
- Sleepless nights

- Hunger (Fasting)

Blessings

- Peace
- Quietness
- Confidence (Assurance)

Points to remember:

- The peaceable fruit of righteousness is found through discipline (chastisement).
- After chastisement, we can be partakers of his holiness.

Memory Verse

I delight greatly in the LORD; my soul rejoices in my God. For he has clothed me with garments of salvation and arrayed me in a robe of righteousness. Isaiah 61:10

CHAPTER NINE

KNOWLEDGE

*Knowledge: Understanding truth through facts
or through reasoning: Cognition.*

1. Exodus 31:3 Who filled this man with artistic knowledge?

2. 2 Chronicles 1 :10 What did Solomon ask of God?

3. Job 36:12 What might happen if we don't listen?

4. A. Psalm 14:4 Who will never learn (or have no knowledge)?

    B. Why do they have no knowledge?

5. A. Psalm 94:10 Who teaches man?

B. How do you think he teaches us?

6. A. Psalm 119:66 What is the psalmist asking God to teach him?

    B. What gives us the motivation to ask for knowledge and good judgment?

7. A. Proverbs 1:4 What is the purpose of Proverbs?

    B. Verse 5. The wise receive what?

    C. What do the discerning receive?

8. A. Proverbs 1:7 What is the beginning of knowledge?

    B. What do fools despise?

9. Proverbs 1:22 What does the Bible call those who hate knowledge?

10. A. Proverbs 1:29 What must we love?

    B. What must we choose?

    C. If time permits outline the verse 24-33

11. Proverbs 2:3 How do we receive insight (knowledge)?

12. Proverbs 2:5 Understanding of what helps us find knowledge?

13. Proverbs 2:6 Where does knowledge come from?

14. Proverbs 2:10 When wisdom enters your heart, what will be pleasant to your soul?

15. Proverbs 8:8-9 The words of God are what to those you have knowledge?

16. Proverbs 8:10 What is better than choice gold?

17. A. Proverbs 10:14 What do wise men do?

    B. What do fools invite?

18. A. Proverbs 12:1 If you love knowledge, you will also love what?

    B. What kind of a person hates correction?

19. A. Hosea 4:6 Why are the people destroyed?

    B. What happens if we reject knowledge?

    C. If we ignore God, who will He ignore?

    20) Romans 1:28 What happens if we don't purpose to retain knowledge?

21) Romans 11:33 How does the Bible describe wisdom and knowledge?

22) A. 1 Corinthians 8:1 What happens if you seek too much knowledge?

B. What can balance knowledge and make it useful?

23) 2 Corinthians 10:5 What can we do with arguments and pretensions (attitude) that set themselves up against the knowledge of God?

24) Ephesians 3:19 What is greater than knowledge?

25) Philippians 3:8 What did Paul count loss to know (to have the knowledge of) Christ?

26) 2 Peter 2:20 How do we escape the corruption of the world?

Answers

1. Spirit of God.
2. Wisdom and knowledge to govern his people.
3. We could perish by the sword or die without knowledge.
4. A. Evildoers (Workers of iniquity)
B. They do not call upon the name of the Lord.
5. A. God.
B. He teaches us through the statutes, precepts, principles and commandments of his Word. He teaches us through historical stories and parables.
He teaches us through preaching.
6. A. Knowledge and good judgment.
B. Our belief
7. A. To give prudence to the simple, knowledge and discretion to the young.
B. Wiser (added to their learning)
C. Guidance.

8. A. Fear of the Lord.

B. Wisdom and discipline

9. Fools

10. A. Knowledge.

B. Fear of the Lord.

11. Call out for insight (knowledge); cry aloud for understanding.

12. Fear of the Lord.

13. Knowledge comes from the mouth of God.

14. Knowledge.

15. Faultless.

16. Knowledge.

17. A. Store up knowledge.

B. Ruin.

18. A. Discipline.

B. A stupid person

19.A. Lack of knowledge

B. God rejects us.

C. Our children

20. We are given over to a depraved mind.

21. Riches

22.A. Knowledge puffs up (prideful)

B. Love

23. We are to demolish arguments and every pretension (vanity) that sets itself up against the knowledge of God.

24. There is a love that surpasses all knowledge and fills us with the fullness of God.

25. Paul suffered the loss of "all things" that he might know (have the knowledge of) Christ.

26. Knowing (having knowledge of) Christ.

Review

1. Who gives us knowledge?
2. What did Solomon ask God to give him?
3. What is better than gold?
4. What kind of a person hates correction?
5. If we reject God's knowledge, what kind of a mind will we possess?
6. What do we need to add to knowledge, so we won't be puffed up?

Prayer

Dear God,

Give us wisdom and knowledge to govern our lives under Christ. Let us take every thought captive that sets itself against Your Word. Help us escape the pollution and the corruption of this world. Let us follow You. Give us the knowledge of Christ. We pray and ask you to give us the knowledge of your will through all spiritual wisdom and understanding. Let us live a life worthy of the Lord. Let us please you in every way. Let us escape the pollution of this world, bear fruit and grow in the knowledge of God (Col. 1:9-10). In Jesus Name, Amen

Outline

With Knowledge

Spirit of God

Fear of the Lord

Wisdom and understanding

Wiser

Guidance

Good judgment

Vision for the future

Blessings for our children

Accepting discipline

Storing up knowledge

Faultless

Ability to demolish vanity in our lives

Filled with the fullness of God

Without Knowledge

Perish by the sword and dies without knowledge

Evildoers

Don't call on God's name

Fools

Reprobate Minds

Stupid

Ruin

Balance

Knowledge and love must go together, or we will become prideful.

Memory Verse

I count all things but loss for the excellency of the knowledge of Christ Jesus, my Lord: for whom I have suffered the loss of all things and do count them but dung, (rubbish) that I may win Christ. Philippians 3:8

CHAPTER TEN

INSTRUCTION

Instruction: Is a direction, calling for compliance;
or an order.

Discipline and Instruction are interchangeable language between the KJV and the NIV translations.

1.   Proverbs 12:1 If you hate instruction what does the Bible call you?

2.   2 Timothy 3:16 Why was Scripture written?

3.   Psalm 50:16-17 A. What kind of a person hates instructions?

     B. How do you know someone doesn't love instructions?

Discussion

What would it look like to cast God's Word behind you?

4.   Proverbs 1:2, 3 Why was proverbs written?

5. Proverbs 1:8 What is your instructions?

6. Proverbs 4:1 What is the instruction?

7. Proverbs 4:13 What are some practical ways to take hold of instruction?

8. Proverbs 5:12-13 What kind of a person has hated discipline and spurned correction? Answer in Verse 13

9. Proverbs 5:22-23 What does this person lack and what happens to them?

10. Proverbs 6:23 A. What is my lamp and light?

B. What should I be asking my mentors?

11. Proverbs 8:10 What is better than silver or gold?

12. Proverbs 8:33 What should I be listening for?

13. Proverbs 9:9 What kind of a person can receive instructions?

14. Proverbs 9:7-8 What happens when you try to instruct (correct) a mocker?

15. Proverbs 10:17 A person who ignores correction leads others where?

16. Proverbs 13:1 Contrast a wise son compared to a scorner.

17. Proverbs 13:18 Contrast one who receives instruction and one who refuses it?

18. Proverbs 15:5 Contrast

19. Proverbs 15:32 Contrast

More verses on Instruction

- Proverbs 15:33 Fear of the LORD teaches (instructs) a man in wisdom.
- Proverbs 16:22 (KJV) Instruction of fools is folly.
- Proverbs 19:20 Advice and instruction make you wise.
- Proverbs 19:27 If you stop listening to instruction, you will stray away from knowledge.
- Proverbs 23:12 Apply your hearts to instruction and your ears to words of knowledge.
- Proverbs 23:23 (KJV) Buy the truth and sell it not; Also, wisdom, and instruction, and understanding.
- Proverbs 24:32 (KJV) Then I saw, and considered it well: I looked upon it, and received instruction.
- Jeremiah 17:23 Yet they did not listen or pay attention; they were stiff-necked and would not listen or respond to discipline (instruction).
- Jeremiah 32:33 They turned their backs to me and not their faces; though I taught them again and again, they would not listen or respond to discipline (instruction).

Answers

1. Stupid. To love instruction is to love.... Knowledge
2. For doctrine, reproof, correction, and instructions in righteousness.
3. A. A wicked person.
   B. They cast God's Words behind them.
4. To give us wisdom and instructions
5. Hear the instruction of your father and do not forsake your mother's teaching.
6. Hear the instruction of your father and pay attention to gain understanding.
7. Answers will vary.
8. Those who refused to obey teachers or hear instructions.

9. Lack of discipline; They may die or be led astray by their own folly.
10. A. The commandments are a lamp. Teaching is a light.
    B. "Give me correction!" "What do you see in my life, that needs to change?"
11. Instruction and knowledge
12. Instruction
13. A wise and righteous person.
14. They insult, abuse, and hate you.
15. This person leads others astray.
16. Wise son hears instructions.
    Scorner refuses to listen.
17. Receiving instruction=honor
    Refusing instruction=poverty and shame
18. Prudent =heeds instruction
    Fool=despises instructions/spurns discipline
19. Refuses instruction=despises own soul.
    Hears reproof=gains understanding

Review

1. What does the Bible call people who hate instruction?
2. How do I receive instruction?
3. What should I always be listening to receive?
4. How can you recognize a mocker?
5. Tell me something about a person who receives instruction?
6. Tell me something about a person who refuses instruction?

Prayer

Dear God,

Help me to love instruction. Help me to listen intently for instructions and to be quick to obey you. Teach me to never cast your Words behind me. Help me to seek after instruction. Help me to humble myself quickly and to receive correction. Give me a heart to study your Word and to know it well enough to guide me and light my path. Give me spiritual ears to hear and discern instructions quickly. In Jesus Name I pray, Amen

Outline

Love Instruction

Knowledge
Receives instruction

Hears father
Pays attention
Obedient
Hears Correction

Blessings

God's Words become a lamp.
Become wise
Honor

Hate Instruction

Wicked- fools
Casts God's Words behind Him.
Lacks discipline
Led astray by their own folly
Refuses to listen
Despises Instruction
Despises his own soul

Behaviors

Insults others
Abuses others
Hates those who correct them.

Consequences

Poverty
Shame
Death

Memory Verse

The instruction (law) of the Lord is perfect, reviving the soul. The statutes of the Lord are trustworthy, making wise the simple. Psalm 19:7

CHAPTER ELEVEN

PRUDENCE

Prudence – *the ability to govern and discipline oneself using reason.*

1. Proverbs 8:12 Who are prudence's best friends?

2. Proverbs 12:16 Contrast fool and prudent.
    Fools-
    Prudent-

3. Proverbs 12:23 Contrast fool and prudent.
    Fools-
    Prudent-

    *Discuss the difference between playing and being overly silly and foolishness.

4. Proverbs 13:16 Contrast fool and prudent.
    Fools-
    Prudent-

Definition of folly: A lack of good sense and insight. Some synonyms for folly are foolishness, stupidity, insanity, madness, nonsense, or absurdity.

5. Proverbs 14:8 Contrast fool and prudent.
   Fools-
   Prudent-

6. Proverbs 14:15 Contrast simple and prudent.
   Simple-
   Prudent-

   Do you think before you speak?
   Do you consider how your actions will affect other people?

7. Proverbs 14:18 Contrast.
   Simple-
   Prudent-

   <u>A crown would be like receiving honor.</u>

8. Proverbs 15:5 Contrast.
   Foolish-
   Prudent-

   A foolish person will speak foolishly about their authority. (Parents, teachers, boss, police, etc.)

9. Proverbs 16:21 What is the wise in heart called?

   How should we give instructions?

10. Proverbs 18:15 Who acquires knowledge?

    A prudent/wise person listens for knowledge.

11. Proverbs 19:14 Who gives you a prudent companion?

SEVEN PILLARS OF WISDOM

12. Proverbs 22:3 Contrast prudent and simple.
    Prudent-
    Simple-

13. Isaiah 5:20-23 Outline twelve "woes" of those with false prudence.

14. Hosea 14:9 The discerning or prudent understand what?

    What do the rebellious do with God's ways?

    Stumble *means they will fall away from God's ways.*

15. Amos 5:13 Sometimes a good person is to speak up. But when times are evil what does a prudent person do?

16. Ephesians 1:8 What is our spiritual blessing in Christ?

17. Ephesians 1:9 What does this blessing make known to us?

18. Ephesians 1:7 What prepares us to know this mystery?

Answers

1. Wisdom, knowledge, and discretion
2. Fool – shows their annoyance (wrath/anger)
   Prudent- overlooks an insult (covers shame)
3. Fools – blurts out folly (foolish act or idea)
   Prudent – keeps knowledge to themself (restrains speech)
4. Fool exposes their folly
   Prudent man acts out of knowledge
5. Fool- folly is deception (deceit)
   Prudent – gives thought to their ways
6. Simple – Believes anything
   Prudent – Gives thought to his steps
7. Simple – inherit folly
   Prudent crowned with knowledge
8. Foolish – Spurns discipline/authority
   Prudent - Accepts correction
9. Discerning (prudent)
   Pleasant words. Give instructions with kindness
10. Discerning (prudent)
11. The Lord
12. Prudent – Sees danger and takes refuge (hides himself KJV)
    Simple – keep going and suffer for it.
13. Call evil good
    And good evil
    Put darkness for light
    Put light for darkness
    Bitter for the sweet
    Sweet for the bitter
    Wise in their own eyes
    Clever (prudent) in their own eyes

Heroes at drinking wine
Champions at drinking strong drink
They acquit (declare innocent) the guilty for a bribe
They deny justice for the innocent

14. They will understand the ways of the LORD are right
    And they will walk in righteousness.
    The rebellious (transgressors) will stumble.
15. Keeps quiet.
16. Wisdom and understanding (prudence).
17. Mystery of His will.
18. Redemption through the blood of Christ.
    Forgiveness of sins.
    Riches of God's grace.

Review

1. Who are prudence's best friends?
2. What is folly?
3. Tell me somethings that fools do?
4. Tell me somethings that the prudent do?
5. How would you recognize someone with false prudence?
6. What prepares me to receive the mystery of God's will?

Prayer

Dear Heavenly Father,

We come before you and understand without your blessing of wisdom, we are fools. Please open our eyes of understanding and discernment that we may possess prudence. Let prudence help us govern and discipline ourselves in righteousness from the Word of God. Helps us to remember that when we are instructing or teaching to do so with gentleness and kindness so others may receive direction from us. Let light pierce the darkness that we may see those with fake prudence that we may not be led astray. Let no simpleton, no foolish peer, or any rebel gain access to our heart or mind. May we be steadfast on your path and never be led astray. In Jesus name we pray, Amen.

Outline

Fools

- Shows annoyance or anger
- Blurt out foolishness

- Exposes folly
- Deceitful
- Spurns/refuses discipline/authority

Simple

- Believes anything
- Inherits folly
- Keep going when they see danger and suffer for it

Prudence

Hangs out with wisdom, knowledge, and discretion

- Overlooks an insult
- Restrains his speech
- Acts out of knowledge
- Gives thoughts to his steps
- Crowned with knowledge
- Accepts correction
- Uses pleasant words
- See danger and hides from it
- He will understand the ways of the LORD
- He will walk in God's ways.
- Keeps quiet when he needs to
- Knows the mystery of God's will
- Receives redemption and forgiveness through the blood of Christ.
- Inherits the riches of God's grace.

False Prudence

- Call evil good
- And good evil
- Put darkness for light
- Put light for darkness
- Bitter for the sweet
- Sweet for the bitter
- Wise in their own eyes
- Clever (prudent) in their own eyes
- Heroes at drinking wine

- Champions at drinking strong drink
- They acquit (declare innocent) the guilty for a bribe
- They deny justice for the innocent

Memory Verse

I, wisdom, dwell together with prudence; I possess knowledge and discretion. Proverbs 8:12

CHAPTER TWELVE

MORE WISDOM

Oh, the depth of the riches of the wisdom and knowledge of God! How unsearchable his judgments, and his paths beyond tracing out! Romans 11:33

1. Proverbs 4:1 What is our job?

   Understanding is knowing the difference between good and evil.

2. Proverbs 4:4 What am I to hear and do? –

   What blessing will I receive if I do this?

3. Proverbs 4:5 What am I not to forget?

4. Proverbs 4:6 What's my blessing if I never forsake wisdom and I love her?

Discussion

If something bad happens to me, does that mean I don't have wisdom?

No, there are other possible reasons for something going amiss in our lives.

1) Hebrews 12:11 Chastening
2) Luke 22:31-32 Strayed away from the path; need to turn back; you have a job to do.
3) Proverbs 24:16 learning perseverance
4) Romans 8:18 suffering common to man

5. Proverbs 4:7 What is the main thing we need?

   What do we need to go along with wisdom?

6. Proverbs 4:8 How are we to honor wisdom?

   What blessings will I receive if I do this?

7. Proverbs 4:9 What is the gift wisdom gives me?

8. Ephesians 1:17 What does Paul pray for his fellow believers who have faith?

9. Ephesians 1:18 What is the second thing Paul prays?

   Why? –

- If we have our eyes open, we will know what a priceless treasure we have in God's Wisdom and how His power gives us strength to change in our daily lives.
-

10. Outline James 3:13–18 True and False Wisdom

True Wisdom

A. What is the FRUIT of true wisdom?

B. Where does true wisdom come from?

False Wisdom

C. What is the FRUIT of false wisdom?

D. What are my INSTRUCTIONS?

E.   Where does false wisdom originate?

F.   Where does true wisdom originate?

11. Proverbs 26:16 Who thinks they are wise and are not?

12. Proverbs 19:8 If a person loves their own soul for what will they search?

>   Soul is defined as my mind, will, and emotions or feelings.
>   It is the part of me that thinks, acts, feels, and guides my decisions.
>   If my soul isn't regenerated by the Holy Spirit, it will deceive me and lead me astray. (Titus 3:5; Jeremiah 17:9)

13. Psalms 119:98 What makes me wiser than my enemies?

14. Proverbs 9:9 What is the way to receive wisdom?

15. Romans 16:19 Are we to be wise in all subjects?

Answers

1. Hear the instruction of our parents/heavenly Father and to know or pay attention to understanding.

    Understanding – knowing the difference between good and evil

2. Let my heart lay hold (retain) His words; Keep His commandments.

    Life.

3. Wisdom, understanding and Words of God's mouth

4. Wisdom will protect (preserve) me and protect me (keep me safe).

5. Wisdom.

    Understanding.

6. Exalt (esteem) her. Embrace her.

    She will exalt (promote) me and bring me honor.

7. She will give me a garland (ornament) of grace and a crown of splendor (glory).

8. Spirit of Wisdom and revelation (understanding) and that we may know (knowledge of) Him (Jesus Christ) better.

9. For the eyes (spiritual eyes) of your heart (understanding) to be enlightened.

    Why? 1) To know the hope of our calling; 2) riches of the glory of the inheritance of the saints and 3) incomparable great power (exceeding greatness) to us who believe.

10. A. Good life (conversation)

    Deeds done in humility with wisdom (works with meekness of wisdom)

        Pure

        Peaceable

        Gentle

        Easy to be entreated

        Full of mercy

        Good fruits without partiality

        And without hypocrisy

        B. Righteousness

        Peace

        C. Heaven

        D. Envy (Bitter envying)

        Selfish ambition (Strife in your hearts)

        E. Disorder (confusion)

        Evil practice (work)

        F. Don't boast

        Don't deny the truth. (Lie not against the truth)

G. Earthly
Unspiritual (sensual)
Of the devil (Devilish)
H. Heaven
11. A sluggard or a lazy man.
12. Wisdom
13. God's commandments (commands).
14. Instruction
15. No, we are to be wise is what is good and innocent (simple) in what is evil.

Review

1. What is my job?
2. What am I not to forget?
4. What is the fruit of earthly wisdom?
5. What is the fruit of heavenly wisdom?
6. Do I need to learn wisdom about evil things?

ACCOUNTABILITY QUESTIONS

1. Am I attentive to my authority: parents, teacher, boss, police, etc.?
2. Am I attentive to the instructions of God's Word?
3. Am I learning, growing, and recognizing the differences between good and evil?
5. Do I make excuses for my willfulness?
6. Do I disrespectfully tell my authorities they are wrong?
7. Do I have a personal quiet devotion time with the Lord to hear His instructions to me?
8. Do I study, meditate, and focus on Scripture daily?
9. Do I obey to my best ability and trust God with the results?
10. Do I look for learning experiences in my life?

Outline

Our Responsibility

Listen and Hear
Be Attentive

Discipline to be in the Word and to grow in wisdom and understanding
Believe
Receive Instruction
Don't be lazy
Be simple concerning evil and wise concerning good

Holy Spirit's Responsibility

Promote me
Give me honor
Give me a garland of grace
Crown of splendor (glory)
Help me to know Christ more
Enlighten my spiritual eyes
Give me a hope in my calling
Show me the riches of the glory of the inheritance in the saints
Give me incomparable great power

Heavenly Wisdom

Good life
Humility
Pure
Peaceable
Gentle
Easy to entreat
Full of mercy
Good fruit without partiality or hypocrisy
Righteousness and Peace

Earthly Wisdom

Envy
Selfish Ambition
Strife/arguments
Disorder/confusion
Evil work
Boasting
Denying the truth

Prayer

Heavenly Father, Grant us this day the ability to hear instructions. Give us wisdom and understanding. Help us seek and find your knowledge. Help us to understand the difference between good and evil and to choose good. Help us to not make excuses for sin but to walk in righteousness and honesty to be the person you desire us to be. Oh, Father help us to be faithful and diligent to study your Word daily.   Let us not miss a single day the rest of our lives. Wake us up with your beautiful commandments in our hearts and singing on our lips. Forgive us for the evil we have learned. Let us purpose to turn away from learning evil and pursue heavenly wisdom from above. Help us to see our own selfishness or laziness and repent quickly.   Help us to recognize strife and arguments as a symptom of earthly, devilish wisdom. Guide us to follow after Wisdom so the fruit of our lives will be peace and right living and your holy name may be glorified. In Jesus Name we pray, Amen.

Memory Verse

I want you to be wise about what is good, and innocent about what is evil. Romans 16:19

DIGGER DEEPER

UNDERSTANDING DEFILEMENT

He who has no rule over his own spirit (lacks self-control) is like a city that is broken down, and without walls. Proverbs 25:28

Introduction

Sponges soak up everything. If we are a sponge, and a person in front of us is angry, we are angry. If they are sad, we are sad. We never really **own** our own emotions but become a chameleon of our environment. Preschoolers are famous for soaking up their emotional atmosphere. They don't possess the maturity not to. *He that is slow to anger is better than the mighty; and he that rules his spirit (controls his temper) than he that takes a city. Proverbs 16:32*

Awareness of defilement is key to maturity. Defilement can be by another person's actions or behaviors and can cause mental captivity where we are stuck in the past. Defiling ourselves is common. The rehearsing of lies uncontrollable circumstances or broken promises produces a heartache. This type of defilement places us in a self-imposed prison. So, we can be defiled by others or ourselves repeatedly. Know the difference. When others defile me, it isn't my fault. I must forgive, then take my pain to the foot of the cross and praise God that He can give me beauty for ashes.

*The Spirit of the Sovereign Lord is on me because the Lord
has anointed me to preach good news to the poor, He has sent me to
bind up the brokenhearted, to proclaim freedom for the captives and
release from darkness for the prisoners, to proclaim the year of the
Lord's favor...to comfort all who mourn... to bestow on them a crown of
beauty instead of ashes, the oil of gladness instead of mourning, and a
garment of praise instead of a spirit of despair...Isaiah 61:1-3*

An emotionally immature person cannot allow you to have your own emotions and comfort you. The sharing of emotional pain irritates, agitates, and frustrates as they soak it up and mirror it back in an exaggerated manner. Other times, they fret on how to fix the problem and give unhelpful advice. Still other folk will pick up an offense and carry it for a decade growling and grumbling about the past injustices done to you; this also, isn't helpful. Then you have the polite people who will pretend to listen and then avoid you like the plague. They don't have the capacity to share your pain either. The result is the same; nothing is resolved, and you are alone and stuck in pain. Find supportive friends who work on understanding themselves and aren't afraid to share in your sufferings.

Lesson

Exercise your spirit to <u>discern good and evil</u>. *But solid food is for the mature, who by constant use have trained themselves to distinguish good from evil. Hebrews 5:14* Today, we will discern the different levels of fools in Proverbs. This will help us identify when we are being defiled or defiling ourselves.

Level One Fool: Naïve
This includes all children and those who have not been properly instructed.
Naïve fool is young, simple and without understanding. They are usually lazy and complacent when it comes to seeking wisdom.
1) **A naïve person is easily led astray and ends up in trouble unintentionally. He is impressionable and doesn't recognize danger.** *A simple (naïve) man believes anything, but a prudent man gives thought to his steps. Proverbs 14:15*
2) **A simple person cannot discern danger.** *A prudent man sees danger and takes refuge, but the simple keep going and suffer for it. Proverbs 22:3*

3) He is on his way to death unless he actively receives tutoring. *For waywardness of the simple will kill them, and the complacency of fools will destroy them.* Proverbs 1:32
4) Folly is a lack of good sense or insight. *The simple inherit folly, but the prudent are crowned with knowledge. Proverbs 14:18*
5) Folly is undisciplined and has no knowledge. The woman, Folly is loud; she is undisciplined and without knowledge. Proverbs 9:13
6) Aimless-but his tempters have an agenda. *My son, if sinners entice you, do not give in to them.* Proverbs 1:10
7) If we refuse to learn, we will graduate to the next level of foolishness. Then, we will be judged in the end. Foolishness rejects God, ignores advice, refuses rebukes...Proverbs 1:24,25 then calamity overtakes you—...disaster sweeps over you like a whirlwind, ...distress and trouble comes upon you...Proverbs 1:27
8) Simple foolishness leads us to be judged if we continue to reject wisdom. *There is a way that seems right to a man, but in the end, it leads to death. Proverbs 14:12*
How do I identify a naivety? • Unguarded • Defenseless • Weak
What other ways can I identify with naivety? • Weak in discernment • Impressionable (Pinocchio) • Follows peers; easily swayed • Unaware of consequences • Open minded and vulnerable to be enticed • Easily drifts into moral corruption • Ends up in trouble
We are to counteract this naivety with accepting instructions and correction. *Hold on to instruction, do not let it go; guard it well, for it is your life. Proverbs 4:13*

Level Two Fool: Stubborn

A stubborn fool is a sign of being governed by the flesh.
This leads to depravity.

<u>Stubborn fool</u> means dull and obstinate. Not slow mentally but slow in wanting to correct themselves and inclined to make wrong decisions because of stubbornness. Stubbornness is one of the greatest character defects!

Characteristics:
- Unrestrained
- Disobedient
- Involved in evil
- Defends actions
- Deceives others
- Covers up motives

Ways to identify a second level fool:
- **Self-confident** *Do you see a man wise in his own eyes? There is more hope for a fool than for him. Proverbs 26:12.*
- **Unreliable** *Like cutting off one's feet or drinking violence is sending of a message by the hand of a fool. Proverbs 26:6*
- **Grief to his parents** *To have a fool for a son brings grief; there is no joy for the father of a fool. Proverbs 17:21*
- **Restless** *A discerning man keeps wisdom in view, but a fool's eyes wander to the end of the earth. Proverbs 17:24*
- **Deceptive and slanderous** *He who conceals his hatred has lying lips, and whoever spreads slander is a fool. Proverbs 10:18*
- **Arrogance** *Arrogant lips are unsuited to a fool—how much worse lying lips to a ruler! Proverbs 17:7*
- **Resentful of correction** *A rebuke impresses a man of discernment more than a hundred lashes a fool. Proverbs 17:10*
- **Un-teachable** *The fear of the Lord is the beginning of knowledge, but fools despise wisdom and discipline. Proverbs 1:7*
- **Opinionated** *A fool finds no pleasure in understanding but delights in airing his own opinions. Proverbs 18:2*
- **Does not prepare his heart to follow wisdom** *Of what use is money in the hand of a fool, since he has no desire to get wisdom. Proverbs 17:16*
- **No reasoning** *Like a lame man's legs that hang limp is a proverb in the mouth of a fool. Proverbs 26:7*

• **Delights to speak evil** *Better a poor man whose walk is blameless than a fool whose lips are perverse. Proverbs 19:1*
• **Mocks sin** *Fools mock at making amends for sin, but goodwill is found among the upright. Proverbs 14:9*
• **Mischief maker** *A fool finds pleasure in evil conduct...Proverbs 10:23*
• **Anger problem** *A fool shows his annoyance at once.* Proverbs 12:16 *A fool gives full vent to his anger. Proverbs 29:11*
• **Provoked easily** *Stone is heavy and sand a burden, but provocation by a fool is heavier than both. Proverbs 27:3*
• **Loss of inheritance** *He who brings trouble on his family will inherit the wind...Proverbs 11:29*
• **Meddling/Quarrelsome** *It is to a man's honor to avoid strife, but every fool is quick to quarrel (meddle). Proverbs 20:3*
• **Reckless and Hotheaded** *A wise man fears the LORD and shuns evil, but a fool is hotheaded and reckless. Proverbs 14:16*
Methods of correcting a Second level fool: • Appeal to him about the consequences of his actions Proverbs 8:5-7; 23:9; 26:4; 29:9 • Do not debate with him Proverbs 26:5 • Restrain him Proverbs 19:29; 26:3 • Don't honor him Proverbs 24:7; 26:1 • Avoid his companionship Proverbs 13:20; 14:7 • Instruct him Proverbs 1:8
Pray: The Holy Spirit convicts us. And empowers us to change. Teach ourselves through the warnings in Scripture. Read Proverbs every day. Correct ourselves. Find accountability partners. Humble ourselves. Educate ourselves so we don't follow a fool or worse...marry a fool!
The end is shame: *The wise inherit honor, but shame shall be the promotion of fools. Proverbs 3:35*

Level Three Fool: Mocker and Scorner

A mocker mocks anyone who won't sin with him, and he mocks anything he doesn't understand. A scorner has snake like venom and is only loyal to himself and will use it on anyone who stands in his way.

Mocker treats others with contempt and ridicule. He defies and challenges authority. He scoffs at purity and righteousness.

A **scorner** openly dislikes, disrespects authority and is indignant with anyone who disagrees with him. He is incorrigible and cannot be directed or taught.

Characteristics:

- Uncontrollable
- Devilish
- Mean Spirited
- Troublemaker
- Bent on corrupting others
- Incorrigible

Hates you *Do not rebuke a mocker, or he will hate you...Proverbs 9:8*

Hates those who correct him *A mocker resents correction; he will not consult the wise. Proverbs 15:12*

Rejects rebuke *A wise son heeds his father's instruction, but a mocker does not listen to rebuke. Proverbs 13:1*

Can't find wisdom *A mocker seeks wisdom and finds none...Proverbs 14:6*

Refuses wisdom and correction *A fool spurns his father's discipline, but whoever heeds correction shows prudence. Proverbs 15:5*

Delights in scorning; hates knowledge *How long will you simple ones love your simple ways? How long will mockers delight in mockery and fools hate knowledge. Proverbs 1:22*

Mocks Justice *A corrupt witness mocks at justice, and the mouth of the wicked gulps down evil. Proverbs 19:28*

Proud/Haughty *Proud and haughty scorner is his name, who deals in proud wrath. Proverbs 21:24*

Contentious *Drive out a mocker, and out goes strife, quarrels and insults are ended. Proverbs 22:10*

Abomination *The schemes of folly are sin, and men detest a mocker. Proverbs 24:9*

Odious (repugnant or hateful) to society *Mockers stir up a city, but wise men turn away anger. Proverbs 29:8*

Methods to correct a mocker/scorner:

- Punish him and the simple will beware. Proverbs 19:25; 21:11
- Give him strong punishments Proverbs 19:29
- Expel him/cast him out Proverbs 22:10
- Expect God to mock him Proverbs 3:34
- He reaps what he sows. Galatians 6:7

Be not deceived; God is not mocked; for whatsoever a man sows, that he shall reap. Galatians 6:7

Exercise

Recognize emotional defilement.
Is it yours?
Does it belong to someone else?
Is it unhealthy?
How can you grow from it?

Application

It is a vital skill to learn the different levels of a fool. I need to identify foolishness within myself and to be wise enough to steer clear of the confusion brought on by fools. I can be defiled by my own foolishness or the foolishness of others. If I learn to recognize it, renounce it, reject it, and live above it, I can stand strong in wisdom and discernment during times of conflict.

My foolishness can be quickly remedied by my diligent determination to respond well to instruction and correction. We have been born fools by default and can only become wise through **intentionality**.

Cure:
- Accept correction immediately while it is small. *Folly is bound in the heart of a child, but the rod of discipline will drive it far from him. Proverbs 22:15*
- Accept instruction and correction. *All scripture is given by inspiration of God, and is profitable for doctrine, for reproof, for correction, for instruction in righteousness. 2 Timothy 3:16*

Warning: He will die without instruction (with lack of discipline); led astray by his own great folly. Proverbs 5:23

Principle

Emotional maturity owns complete responsibility to receive instructions and correction.

Conclusion

Until we own our own inner spirit, our own thoughts, and think the thoughts we want to think, we are governed by the noise of those around us. Govern your inner self by intentionally developing an ear that listens for instruction and correction. I cannot trust my own ways, so I trust God's ways and I repeatedly speak the Word of God to myself to break the habitual patterns of immature behaviors.

Defilement Recovery Questionnaire:	
Mark 1-10 (10 is doing the best I can do.)	
1) How well do I receive instructions?	
2) Am I listening intently for instructions?	
3) How easily can I be corrected?	
4) Can I take correction without being offended?	
5) Can I humble myself and ask a trusted friend/mentor for correction?	
6) How well can I recognize foolish behavior (mine and others)?	
7) What behaviors do I need to correct?	
8) Name some of the things that have been said to defile you and renounce them. Examples: You are stupid. You will never amount to anything. You can't you do anything right?	
9) Name some of the things that have been done to you and renounce their power over you. Mocked, ridiculed, made to feel dumb, humiliated, abused verbally, physically, financially. Abandoned, neglected, misunderstood, rejected...	

1 John 4:4 You, dear children, are from God and have overcome them, because the one who is in you is greater than the one who is in the world.

Romans 8:37 *No, in all these things we are more than conquerors through him who loved us. For I am convinced that neither death nor life, neither angels nor demons, neither the present nor the future, nor any powers, neither height nor depth, nor anything else in all creation, will be able to separate us from the love of God that is in Christ Jesus our Lord.*

Look for it as for silver and search for it as for hidden treasure Proverbs 2:4
Contrast Wisdom (understanding, discernment, truth...) and Foolishness (pride arrogance, stubbornness...)

FIND 25 INSTRUCTIONS
IN PROVERBS

1)

2)

3)

4)

5)

6)

7)

8)

9)

10)

11)

12)

13)

14)

15)

16)

17)

18)

19)

20)

21)

22)

23)

24)

25)

FIND 25 WARNINGS
FROM PROVERBS

1)

2)

3)

4)

5)

6)

7)

8)

9)

10)

11)

12)

13)

14)

15)

16)

17)

18)

19)

20)

21)

22)

23)

24)

25)

CHALLENGE ONE

PRAYING SCRIPTURES

Turn the Scriptures in Proverbs around and pray them. Write out ten.

CHALLENGE TWO

SECRET INSIGHT

Read a chapter in Proverbs every day of the month and find one verse and write it out and meditate on it all day and discover a secret insight in the verse.

Day One Insight:

Day Two Insight:

Day Three Insight:

Day Four Insight:

Day Five Insight:

Day Six Insight:

Day Seven Insight:

Day Eight Insight:

Day Nine Insight:

Day Ten Insight:

Day Eleven Insight:

Day Twelve Insight:

Day Thirteen Insight:

Day Fourteen Insight:

Day Fifteen Insight:

Day Sixteen Insight:

Day Seventeen Insight:

Day Eighteen Insight:

Day Nineteen Insight:

Day Twenty Insight:

Day Twenty-One Insight:

Day Twenty-Two Insight:

Day Twenty-Three Insight:

Day Twenty-Four Insight:

Day Twenty-Five Insight:

Day Twenty-Six Insight:

Day Twenty-Seven Insight:

Day Twenty-Eight Insight:

Day Twenty-Nine Insight:

Day Thirty Insight

CHALLENGE THREE

BLESSING

Learn to speak blessings over yourself and family.
Write out five blessings.

CHALLENGE FOUR

BE YOUR OWN CHEERLEADER

Learn to preach to yourself and be your own cheerleader.
Write ten gracious, kind and affirming words to yourself.

CHALLENGE FIVE

WRITE YOUR OWN STUDY

Choose a word from Proverbs that intrigues you and look up all the references to it and its synonyms in Proverbs. Then, write ten questions on the topic. Place your answers at the bottom and share your study with your friends and family. At the end, write what you think the Lord is saying about this topic to you. If you can't find ten verses on your topic, venture out into the Psalms or other books of the Bible. You can also look your word up in different versions of the Bible.

Abomination
Afflict, affliction, suffer
Anger, angry
Argue, contention, brawler
Bless, blessing
Bread
Comfort
Confidence
Cry, crying, crying out
Darkness/dark/obscure
Day/Night
Death/hell
Desire
Desolation/destruction
Despair
Destroy

Dishonor/honor
Distress
Dogs
Dominion
Ear/Listen
Eye/Seeing
Earth
Eat
Enemy
Everlasting
Evil
Excellent
Faint
Faith/faithful
Fall
Father
Fear, Afraid,
Feet
Folly
Forsake/forsaken
Friend
Give
Glory
Good
Gossip,
Hand
Hard, harden, hardness
Heart
Heaven
Humble/Humility/Humbly
Idolatry/Witchcraft
Iniquity
Joy/rejoice
King
Learn
Life
Love
Mercy
Name
Oppress/oppression

Peace
Quiet/quietly/quietness
Redeem/redeemer/redemption
Refuse
Remember
Reproach
Reprove
Rest
Return
Reward
Rich
Right/righteous/righteousness
Rock
Sacrifice
Safety
Saint
Salvation
Seek
Shadow
Sin/sinner
Sloth/Lazy
Sorrow
Soul
Spirit/spiritual/spiritually
Stand
Strength/strengthen
Strong
Thought
Tongue, slander, backbiting,
Trap/snare
Treasure
Trust
Trouble
Trust
Upright
Voice
Walk
Way
Wicked
Word

CHALLENGE SIX

OUTLINE ONE CHAPTER IN PROVERBS

Pick the main word in each verse.
Can you find a theme in the chapter?
Find the warnings, cautions, instructions, promises, etc.

AUTHOR'S BIOGRAPHIES

Angie Meadows graduated from St Mary's School of Nursing as a Registered Nurse, Marshall University with a Bachelor's in Nursing and Ohio State University with a Master's in Nursing. She is a self-taught Bible student. Angie homeschooled her children for 23 years and taught Children's Sunday School and Women's Bible studies for decades. She loves inspiring others to love the Lord and seek a closer relationship with Him. She is currently a mother, grandmother, speaker, and writer. Her favorite pastime is quilting and discipling others. Angie manages an Extended Sober Living support house and volunteers teaching and disciplining in Recovery Houses.

OTHER RESOURCES BY THE AUTHOR

Enabler/Addiction Recovery Materials:

1) A Thousand Tears: An Enabler's Journey
2) An Enabler's Journey: A Christian Perspective
3) Enabler's Journey Recovery Plan: Enabler's Journey Recovery Series Book One
4) Enabler's Journey Detachment: Enabler's Journey Recovery Series Book Two
5) Rock of Recovery Anxiety Trap
6) Rock of Recovery Overcoming Torment
7) Rock of Recovery Overcoming Trauma
8) Rock of Recovery Spirit and Soul Disconnect

Small Group 12 Lesson Bible Study
Developmental Emotional Maturity Skills

9) Rule and Reign Your Internal World: Defeating Anxiety

rockofrecovery.com Website has John/Romans Verse by Verse Bible Study and other studies posted regular.

Kindle eBooks available for all title.

www.ingramcontent.com/pod-product-compliance
Lightning Source LLC
Chambersburg PA
CBHW060023050426
42448CB00012B/2853